THE SEVEN LAWS OF THE HARVEST

THE SEVEN LAWS OF THE HARVEST

This is a series of messages Bro Dave preached from the pulpit of Maranatha Baptist Church. A look at some of God's unchanging laws

By Bro Dave Noffsinger

LAW ONE:
WE REAP ONLY WHAT HAS BEEN SOWN
Galatians 6:7-8

Usually, when we think of the concept of reaping what we sow, we think of it in a negative sense. We think of suffering for sinful actions or foolish choices. However, the laws of the harvest have a positive side, too. There is a promise of blessing for sowing that which is good, as well as a warning against sowing what is bad. Look again at our text.

> *"Be not deceived, God is not mocked: for whatsoever a man soweth, that shall he also reap.* **For he that soweth to his flesh shall reap corruption; but he that soweth to the Spirit shall of the Spirit reap everlasting life."**

We can sow the things of the flesh or the things of the Spirit. The one reaps corruption – things that cannot even endure for time. The other reaps benefits that last for eternity.

Life is filled with choices. The decisions we make and those that others make affect us everyday. Choices are important. They can have a life-changing impact. Sometimes we see the effects immediately. At other times, we don't feel the results for years, but **the Laws of the Harvest cannot be avoided**. No man will mock God by setting aside even one of these laws.

All of life is built upon the labor and sowing of others. Someone naturally, purposely, or inadvertently sowed that which we reap. Sometimes the results are positive. Sometimes they are negative. In other words, this law of the harvest, *We Reap Only What Has Been Sown*, has both a positive and a negative side.

1. The Positive Side

A. **Blessings we reap because of what God has sown**

1. The Blessings of providence.
    a. **Matthew 5:45.** Take special note of the pronouns in this verse. It is *His* sun. *He* causes it to shine upon the world; *He* makes it rain - not on the good and deserving only, but on the evil and undeserving, too.
    b. **Acts 17:24-25.** God gives to men every essential of existence: life, breath, and *"all things."* All men live by the grace and goodness of a benevolent Creator.

2. The Blessing of Salvation.
    a. **John 3:16.** God took the initiative to redeem sinful humanity by giving His son in payment for the penalty of sin.

b. **Ephesians 2:8-9.** Whether or not men receive the gift, it is there for the taking.

B. Blessings we reap because of what others have sown

1. **Personally**, we benefit from the contributions others have made into our lives.
   a. Think of those who have instructed, encouraged, and challenged you, building good things into your life.
   b. If we have the opportunity to succeed and excel, others have made it possible.

Illustration

A young woman tells of an experience that forever changed her outlook on life. She was in the sixth grade, and it was the day for end-of-the-year parent/teacher conferences. One by one, the other children and their parents were called into the office to meet with the teacher, but this little girl's parents never came. They hadn't cared enough to come. At last, it was her turn. She entered the office and sat with head bowed, embarrassed that her parents were not there. Then her teacher spoke the words the girl would never forget. She said, "First, I want you to know that I love you. Next, I want you to know that it isn't your fault that your parents didn't show up. Third, you are a great student and deserve to have your work reviewed." Then the teacher began to give that girl the same time and attention which she had given every other student. In so doing, she gave her a dose of self-esteem that has sustained her well into her adult years.

2. **Nationally**, we owe a great debt to those who have given us a free and prosperous country in which to live.
a. How different would life in America be if our forefathers had not founded this nation on Christian principles?
b. How many of our freedoms would have been lost if men had not been willing to fight and die to preserve them?

3. **Spiritually**, we would not enjoy the privileges of our Christian faith if it were not for the faithfulness of others.
a. What if someone had not cared enough to share the gospel with you?
b. What if others had failed to obey the Great Commission and plant churches all over America?

2. The Negative Side

A. **We reap the wrong others have sown**

1. We all reap the sin of Adam. Romans 5:12

a. When Adam sinned, he made all men subject to
sin – its power and its penalty.
b. His sin also caused the earth to be cursed, so
that we must live with sickness, suffering,
hardship, and death.

2. We reap sorrow and suffering from the sins and
failures of our family.

a. Numbers 14:18. The consequences of sin can be
passed on to several generations.
b. Ezekiel 18:2-3. A father cannot sin
without hurt to his family.
c. Proverbs 17:25. When a child rebels and makes
foolish choices, he grieves his parents.

3. We reap the wrong of foolish or corrupt leaders and
the effects of living in a godless society.

a. Rom 1:21-32. When a generation abandons its
faith in God and turns to humanistic philosophies
and pagan religion, all of society suffers.
b. Proverbs 29:2.

B. **We reap the wrong we have sown**

1. God is willing to forgive us our sins, but we cannot always escape the consequences.

2. Although a man may hide, excuse, or ignore his sins, he will reap the effects of his behavior – in the form of suffering, guilt, or the judgment of God. Numbers 32:23

3. The Law Applied

A. Consider the harvest before you sow.

1. What will be the results of your choices? To yourself? To others?

a. We reap only what has been sown. Someone will be effected by your choices.
b. We cannot escape the fact that we have a responsibility to others.

THINK ABOUT IT: If we only reap the blessings and fail to sow good things back into the lives of others, then the next generation will not know the blessings we have enjoyed. See Deut. 6:10-12

2. Are you sowing anything that will bear eternal fruit?

a. Only one thing upon the earth that will outlast the earth: the souls of men.

b. Every Christian needs to be involved in some way in personally winning others to Christ. See Mark 8:35

    - There is a harvest to be reaped for our bus ministry.

    - There are families to be reached for Christ.

    - The fields are white unto harvest. All that is lacking is reapers.

B. **Be thankful to those who have sown so that you could reap good things.**

1. Thank God for His blessings.
2. Don't abuse the blessings passed on to us by others through ingratitude or indifference.

C. **Realize that God's grace is greater than the negative things we reap.**

1. Past offenses can be forgiven and the effects of bitterness put away.
2. As Christians, we can rest assured that when we have godless rulers or must endure hard times, God will sustain and care for His children. See Psalm 37:10-13,22-26

LAW TWO:
WE REAP THE SAME IN KIND AS WE HAVE SOWN
2 Samuel 12:9-10

One of the fundamental laws of nature is that we reap the same in kind as we have sown. If a farmer plants wheat, he will harvest wheat – not barley, corn, oats, or anything else – only wheat. The man who plants a pecan orchard will not see oranges, apples, pears, or any other fruit on the branches of his trees. Whatever is harvested will be *like* that which was planted.

The same is true in the realm of human and spiritual relationships. King David is an excellent example of this. He had sown sexual lust and murder; he would reap the same in the lives of his children. The sword, symbolic of violence, would never cease to be associated with his house. **Although forgiven, his sin would continue to produce fruit in the lives of others for many generations**.

However, this law is also positive. Imagine what life for a farmer would be like if he never knew what the seed he planted was going to produce. Suppose he planted wheat, but the seed produced Johnson grass instead? Yet, we know that will never happen. God's second law of the harvest prevents it. In the same way, you and I can be sure that when we sow good seed, we will reap a good harvest in the lives of others.

1. The Foundation for this Law.

A. **The principle of natural reproduction** (Genesis 1:11, 12, 21-25)

1. At creation, God ordered everything to reproduce *"after his kind."*

    a. Fish do not become reptiles.

    b. Monkeys do not become men.

2. This principle has never been broken – not in life, and not in the laboratory.

B. **The principle of spiritual reproduction** (John 3:3-6)

1. What is born of the flesh can never reproduce spiritual life any more than plant life can evolve into animal life.

    a. When Adam disobeyed God and sinned in the garden, he reaped the consequences of his action: spiritual death – the loss of fellowship and relationship with God.

    b. As a sinner, Adam could only reproduce children who would likewise be sinners.

        - Psalm 51:5. When the psalmist states that he was conceived in sin, he was acknowledging that he was born a sinner with a predisposition towards sin.

- Job 15:14-16. Job understood that man is born a sinner and has a "thirst" for sin.

c. Apart from divine intervention, Adam's sin prevented man from reaping any spiritual fruit!

2. By receiving God's gift of salvation, man experiences a spiritual birth (*"born of the Spirit"*) with a new capacity to bear spiritual fruit.

a. When men reject God's salvation and "sow" the seeds of their fallen nature, society always experiences moral degeneration and decay. SEE GALATIANS 6:8a.

b. The Christian who cooperates with the Holy Spirit and bears His fruit reproduces godliness and reaps eternal benefits. SEE GALATIANS 6:8b.

2. The Proclamation of this Law (Galatians 6:7-8)

A. **It is introduced with a warning.** *"Be not deceived, God is not mocked"*

1. Deception can come from two sources.

a. **The devil** actively attempts to blind men to God's truth and the consequences of sin. 2 Corinthians 4:4; Colossians 2:8

b. **We deceive ourselves** when we ignore the truth that we have received or think that God will not hold us accountable for the choices we make or the things we do.

2. God will not be mocked. God does not permit anyone to disregard his principles and live as he pleases and escape the consequences.

B. **It is explained as an absolute.** *"Whatsoever a man soweth, that shall he also reap"*
1. The word *whatsoever* makes this law **all-inclusive**. <u>It applies to anything and everything we sow.</u>
2. The words *that ... also* declares that we will reap the same IN KIND as we have sown.
   a. This law is POSITIVE in that:
   - If we sow of the Spirit, we shall reap of the Spirit.
   - If we sow the Gospel, we will reap converts.
   - If we sow biblical instruction into the lives of our children, we will reap godly character from their lives.
   b. This law is NEGATIVE in that:
   - If we sow to the flesh, we shall reap carnality.
   - If we sow evil, we will reap evil.
   - If we sow indifference to God and godly priorities, we will reap coldness, insensitivity, apathy, and hardness of heart.

3. Illustrations of this Law from Scripture

A. **From the Psalms**

1. Psalm 1:1-6.

   a. The person who shuns the counsel and company of the world and sows the Word of God into his life will reap a blessed and fruitful life.

   b. The person who sows ungodliness will reap an unstable life and the condemnation of God.

2. Psalm 5:10-11

   a. Those who reject God's counsel will be destroyed by their folly; those who persist in sin will reap the fruit of their activities.

   b. The person who sows an attitude of faith (marked by obedience and trust) will reap a season of rejoicing.

3. Psalm 7:15-16. Those who sow deception and prey off the lives of others will eventually be caught by their own devices.

B. **From the Proverbs**

1. Proverbs 11:18

   a. Those who sow wickedness employ themselves in a deceitful work – it promises one thing, but delivers something else.

   b. Those who sow righteousness reap a **sure** reward – they will not be disappointed with the fruit of their labor.

2. Proverbs 22:8a. Another verse that declares that sin does not deliver the satisfaction it advertises.

3. Proverbs 26:27.

C. **From the Words of Christ**
1. Matthew 5:7-8
   a. The one that sows mercy will reap mercy.
   b. The one who sows purity will reap fellowship with God.
2. Luke 6:37-38
   a. If we sow judgment, we will reap criticism.
   b. If we sow condemnation, we will reap rejection.
   c. If we sow forgiveness, we will reap forgiveness.
   d. Verse 38 declares that whatever we give, IT shall be returned to us.
3. Mark 8:35
   a. The Christian who lives for selfish purposes (whether for wealth, influence, comfort, or success) will reap a wasted life. Thinking he "saved" his life for his own use, he will actually "lose" the value of it for all eternity.
   b. The Christian who lives for the sake of Christ and the Gospel, though he may forfeit certain things right now that men value, he will actually preserve the value of his life for all eternity.

APPLICATION:

- In the church, we will reap exactly what we have sown. If we are concerned for lost souls and witness for Christ, we can expect to see souls saved and families added to the church. If we are not seeing souls saved, there can only be one reason: we have not been sowing the Gospel as we should. To say otherwise would be to be deceived.
- In our lives, we reap the values, attitude, and character that we have sown.

LAW THREE:
WE REAP IN A DIFFERENT SEASON THAN WE SOW
Ecclesiastes 3:1-11

There are 31 references to time in this section. First, Solomon declares, *"To everything there is a season."* A **season** refers to **an appropriate period.** You don't plant vegetables in the winter. It's inappropriate. Birds don't build their nests and lay their eggs when the snow is falling. It's the wrong season. This world in which we live works according to a plan. A farmer knows that he must cooperate with nature if he wants to be successful. In the same way, men must adhere to God's principles if they want their lives to prosper.

Additionally, Solomon declares that to everything there is a ***time***. Not only is there an appropriate period, but there is also an **appointed moment.** *"There is a time to be born..."* When it is time for birth to commence, you can't slow it down or put it off. The appointed moment has arrived. That, too, is according to God's design. In the normal course of events, babies are not born too soon, or too late. Crops mature and ripen according to God's schedule. Everything in our lives is governed by **time.**

Solomon observed that there is a time for sowing, and a time for reaping. (Verse 2) As we have already learned, **there is no reaping without sowing** and **what we reap is determined by what we sow.** Today, we are going to see that **we always reap later than we sow.** This is what is sometimes so deceptive about life. If we do not see the immediate results of our actions, we may become discouraged and give up a good activity, such as soulwinning. Or, we may think we got away with a bad choice or a sinful action – not realizing that having sown the seed of sin, we will reap the consequences at point in the future. God will not be mocked. Having sown, we will reap – but **in a different season.**

1. The Foundation of this Law

A. The creative purpose of God – Genesis 8:22

1. The seasons of life cannot be ignored.
God has ordained that summer and winter, seedtime and harvest, and night and day will not cease to occur in their normal cycles as long as the earth remains.
2. This promise of God has both a positive and a negative impact upon our lives.
> a. Positively, we know that God has a rewarding day to acknowledge the service we have done for Christ. 1 Corinthians 15:58
> b. Negatively, we know that we will eventually have to "pay" for the choices we make. It doesn't work to sow our wild oats and then pray for crop failure. Galatians 6:7

B. The "in due season" principle

1. The harvest never comes immediately.
   a. The time between sowing and reaping will vary.
   - You can plant a kernel of corn and be eating ears of corn in a matter of weeks.
   - It takes years for a pecan to sprout, grow, and develop into a tree that produces more pecans.
   b. This is what can make life seem so deceptive. READ PSALMS 73:12-17. The psalmist, Asaph, saw that the ungodly appeared to *"prosper"* and the godly seemed to suffer. When he tried to reconcile this difference with the truth of a wise and just Creator, it was *"too painful"* for him – he couldn't make any sense to him. It SEEMED as if the ungodly were able to sow the seeds of sin and reap the good life … until Asaph *"understood **their end**."* God had to remind Asaph that the season of reaping had not yet arrived for the ungodly.

2. In due season – at the appropriate, appointed time – men will reap that which they have sown, whether good or bad.
   a. Deuteronomy 32:35 - To me *belongeth* vengeance, and recompense; their foot shall slide *in due time…*
   b. Psalm 145:15 – The eyes of all wait upon thee, and thou givest them their meat *in due season.*
   c. Galatians 6:9 – And be not weary in well doing, for *in due season* we shall reap if we faint not.

d. 1 Peter 5:6 - Humble yourselves therefore under the mighty hand of God, that he may exalt you *in due time*.

2. Considerations of this Law

A. **We must not be deceived because the season of harvest is put off.**

We are tempted to think that if consequences of sin do not come quickly, we have escaped God's laws and are free to continue to sin. Ecclesiastes 8:11.

1. **We must remember that what is sown in one season is reaped in another**.
- No one was ever hospitalized for lung cancer the day after he smoked his first cigarette.
- A girl is not sitting in an abortion clinic or delivering a baby the morning after she has yielded her body outside the holy bonds of marriage.
- No one ever went to jail for tax evasion the day they mailed a falsified tax return.

2. **No harvest comes the moment the seed is planted. It must wait for God's appointed time**.

a. God is longsuffering towards sinners and doesn't always punish our sins immediately.

b. However, it is a mistake to look upon God's mercy as though it were ignorance.

B. **We must not be discouraged because the season of harvest is delayed**.

1. We live in a day of instant gratification.
   a. We have instant tea, quick oats, Minute-Brand rice, microwave popcorn, and "no payments for six months" credit purchases.
   b. We can cross town in a few minutes, cross the state in a few hours, and circle the world in just a couple of days.
   c. We watch deep personal conflicts resolved in one-hour dramas.

2. We tend to be an impatient people who want to see the results of our efforts immediately.
   a. A bus route, a Sunday school class, or a church is not built over night.
   b. Strong marriages take a long-term commitment to build.
   c. It takes years of faithful instruction to train our children and build godly character into their lives.

All through life, we are confronted with this truth: we reap in a different season than we sow. We must not allow ourselves to become discouraged and quit while waiting to see the results of our labor.

3. Applications of this Law

A. **We must sow with patience**.
James 5:7-8 reminds us, *Be patient therefore, brethren, unto the coming of the Lord. Behold, the husbandman waiteth for the precious fruit of the earth, and hath long patience for it, until he receive the early and latter rain. Be ye also patient; stablish your hearts: for the coming of the Lord draweth nigh.*

B. **We must wait with patience for the Lord to reward our service**.
   1. Because of His goodness – Psalm 27:13-14
   2. Because of His justice – Proverbs 20:22
   3. Because of His faithfulness – Isaiah 40:27-31
      a. He never becomes discourage; He never grows weary of doing good.
      b. In the weakness of our humanity, He gracefully demonstrates His power and imparts His strength.

Many missionaries have faithfully spread the seed of God's Word and yet had to wait long periods before the season of reaping. William Carey labored 7 years before the first Hindu convert was brought to Christ in India. Adoniram Judson also toiled 7 years before his witness was rewarded with a soul won in Burma. In western Africa, it took 14 years to win the first soul to Christ. In New Zealand, it took 9 years; and in Tahiti, it was 16 years before the first harvest of souls began. However, in each case, **in due season**, souls were won and churches were established.

LAW FOUR:
WE REAP MORE THAN WE SOW
Mark 4:1-8 (esp. Verse 8)

In this parable, Jesus said that the seed that fell on good ground *increased* (verse 8). A single grain grew to be a plant that produced thirty, sixty, or a hundred more seeds. Reaping more than we sow is fundamental to the laws of the harvest. Every farmer lives by this principle. If his work only returned exactly what he had planted in the ground, his labor would be futile. He would never gain anything extra with which to feed his family or sell for a profit. For example, consider the potential of one kernel of corn. **One kernel** of corn will produce **one corn stalk**. On the average, each stalk will produce **three ears**. The average ear of corn has **250 kernels,** so that <u>a single kernel of corn will yield a *750% increase*</u>. **The harvest is always greater than the seed planted –** whether we are speaking of agriculture or the things of our lives. We invariably reap more than has been sown. This fact is both serious and sobering, and it applies equally to the Christian and the unbeliever. Whatever a person sows, whether good or bad, he will reap the benefits or the consequences in a significantly greater proportion.

Of course, there are exceptions to this law because we live in a fallen world. A farmer may have his crops destroyed by drought, and we know that bad things can happen to good people. But even in these instances, God's law is not set aside. If we look at the whole of a life, or all the seasons of harvest, we will find that as a general principle, we reap the same in kind as we have sown (Law 2) and we reap more than we have sown

1. Biblical Expressions of this Law

A. Proverbs 22:8 *"He that soweth iniquity shall reap vanity..."*

1. *Vanity* is from a Hebrew word that is also translated "iniquity," "wickedness," "affliction," or "mischief."
   a. Whereas the word translated *iniquity* emphasizes the deed done, the word translated *vanity* emphasizes the consequences.
   b. Twice (in Deuteronomy 26:14 and Hosea 9:4) it is translated as a form of "mourning" and is associated with death.
2. This verse is telling us that when a person sows iniquity or unrighteousness, they reap adversity and sorrow.

B. Hosea 8:7a *"For they have sown the wind, and they shall reap the whirlwind...."*

1. *Whirlwind* represents the harvest in **kind** (Law 2) that comes from sowing the wind. But it also represents the concept of **more**.

2. A *whirlwind* is a violent, or fierce, wind – such as a tornado.

    a. Israel's expression of displeasure with God (by turning to idols and foreign nations for help) is viewed as a "wind."

    b. God's displeasure and resulting judgment is pictured as a *whirlwind*. The idea is that you may sow a breeze, but you'll reap a gale.

C. Luke 6:38 *"Give, and it shall be given unto you; good measure, pressed down, shaken together, and running over...."*

1. Jesus doesn't specify what is to be given (or sown). However, He does promise that whatever we give, we shall receive *IT* (the same in kind) back again, but more abundantly.

2. A similar promise is made in Malachi 4:10 concerning the tithe – a blessing returned so great that there will not be room enough to receive it.

2. Illustrations of this Law

A. David (2 Samuel 12:9-12)

David is a well-known example of this law from a negative perspective. He sowed iniquity and he reaped trouble. What he began as a little wind blew through his house like a whirlwind. Let's look at the consequences of David's sin. Carefully note how he reaped the same in kind and much more than he sowed.

> 1. David defiled one's man wife. As a result, one of his daughters was raped by her stepbrother and his son Absolom defiled many of his wives.
> 2. David had one man murdered. In time, four of his sons died premature deaths, three of them by violence – the illegitimate child, Amnon, Absolom, and Adonijah.
> 3. David sinned secretly. The consequences he suffered happened openly.

B. The Widow of Zarephath (1 Kings 17:8-16)
1. When Elijah came to the widow's house, she only had a *"handful of meal in a barrel and a little oil in a cruse,"* enough for one meager meal.
2. When she "sowed" it in obedience to the Lord's command, she reaped a continuous supply of meal and oil that fed Elijah and her family for *"many days."*
3. What she gave was given back to her in abundant measure as God had promised. Compare to Luke 6:38.

C. Jesus and the Disciples

1. Jesus selected twelve men and for three years "sowed" the majority of his instruction and example into their lives.

a. Though Christ ministered to the multitudes, he was never with any group of people very long other than his disciples.

b. He kept them with him, taught them privately, and entrusted them with implementing and fulfilling the Great Commission.

c. When Christ was killed, it was assumed that the little movement he had initiated would die with Him.

2. In Ephesians 2:19-20, Paul states that the *household of God* (the church) is built upon the foundation of the apostles.

a. The entire Christian movement grew up out of the ministry of those twelve men (including Paul).

b. The seed planted by Jesus is still producing fruit today as the Gospel continues to go out throughout our world in obedience to the Great Commission.

3. Along the same lines, Hebrews 2:10 states that God sacrificed his **One <u>S</u>on** in order to bring **many <u>s</u>ons** into glory.

3. Applications of this Law (See 1 Corinthians 15:58)

    A. **The time we spend in evangelism is not in vain**. God has sent us to reap (John 4:38) and he will use our witness to win others to Christ.

    B. **The time we invest in service is not in vain**. We never know how God will use our words or acts of service to influence others.

In 1867, an old preacher by the name of Henry Varley led a prayer meeting in London. Not many remember him, but one night he challenged the small crowd who came to his service with this thought: "The world has yet to see what God can do with one man wholly committed to him." A discouraged young preacher by the name of Dwight L. Moody was present that night. He took the words to heart and was greatly used of God for the next 32 years to win thousands to Christ. A little seed was sown, and the harvest was great.

In 1850, a snowstorm struck the town of Colchester, England. On Sunday morning, the snow was so deep that it was nearly impossible to get around. Only a handful of people managed to make it to the Methodist chapel, and the pastor was not one of them. One deacon was present – a tall, thin, frail looking man. He at first considered sending the few people away, but decided it was his duty to give them something from the Scripture. He chose as his text Isaiah 45:22, *"Look unto me, and be ye saved, all the ends of the earth."* For about 10 minutes he rambled on, doing the best he could. Then he happened to notice a young man sitting near the back. "Young man, you look very miserable, and you will always be miserable – miserable in life, miserable in death – until you obey this text. Young man, look to Jesus Christ. You have nothing to do but to look and live." The young man responded to the earnest appeal and accepted Christ. He was sixteen, and his name was Charles Haddon Spurgeon.

Each of these unknown, faithful men of God sowed a tiny seed of service, and reaped a harvest that far exceeded their wildest imagination. They are modern examples of the "much more" principle of this Law of the Harvest. You may not think you have much talent or ability, but if you will dedicate what you have to the Lord and let Him "sow" it where He will, you, too, may be surprised at the abundance you will reap in return.

   C. **The time we spend "sowing the wind" of iniquity is always in vain.**

     1. It brings trouble and sorrows into our lives.

     2. It often brings trouble and sorrow into the lives of our family members and friends.

CONCLUSION: Remember this principle: the harvest is always greater than the seed planted, whatever it may be.

LAW FIVE:
WE REAP IN PROPORTION TO WHAT WE SOW
2 Corinthians 9:6

Both Law Four and Law Five deal with QUANTITY. The **fourth law** states that we reap more than we sow. For example, a farmer can plant about 1 2/3 bushels of barley per acre and he will reap about 54 bushels per acre. By the design of God, the seed sown is multiplied many times. <u>The farmer has nothing to do with it</u>. However, **the fifth law** – We Reap in Proportion to What we Sow – **deals with human responsibility**. If the farmer only planted 1 bushel per acre, his harvest would be considerably smaller. God determines how much the seed is multiplied. The farmer determines how much seed he will sow.

In the area of Christian living, this law tests our faith. It tells us that **how much we receive rests with us**. If we sow sparingly, we will reap sparingly. If we sow bountifully, we will reap bountifully. This is God's law. It is not telling us what *might* happen, but what always occurs. With confidence in God's wisdom, love, and ability, our challenge is to sow to the fullest of our potential and leave the results to God. The more good we sow, the more God can bless our lives with good things.

1. The Background to this Law

A. **We have a moral and spiritual responsibility to be generous**. Proverbs 11:24-26

1. God created within our world a principle of giving.
    a. Every part of creation is designed to give for the good of the other parts.
    - A *tree* draws from the soil and from the air those things it needs to produce oxygen, timber, shade, and fruit.
    - The *earth* gives of its riches and resources to other living things.
    - The *sun* contributes its heat, energy, and even vitamin "D" for our nourishment.

    b. The continuance of life depends upon each part of creation generously, unselfishly giving that which God designed it to give.

2. Man and society are not exempt from this law.
    a. Scattering yields increase; hoarding (withholding *more than is meet*) results in poverty.
    b. Generous people, whatever they give, are "made fat" – they flourish in soul and substance; and they are "watered" – meaning that **you cannot give without receiving**.

c. Those who withhold what others need are cursed while those who make it available are cheered. (Verse 26)

3. At whatever point we fail to give, both we and others suffer.

   a. If the farmer refuses to plant his seed, the economy will suffer.

   b. If a father is stingy with his time at home, his family will suffer.

   c. When Christians fail to share the gospel, the church begins to die and those without Christ suffer.

3. Everywhere we practice generosity, both we and others will thrive. H.A. Ironside writes: **"No one ever loses by loving, nor becomes poor by giving."**

B. **We reap according to the amount we sow.** Luke 6:38b *"For with the same measure...."*

1. This not only applies to finances, but also to everything we have to give – forgiveness, love, ministry and every area of human need.

2. The place to begin sowing is the place where we feel the greatest need.

a. If we are lacking in wisdom of God's Word, invest more time in reading and study.

b. If souls are not being saved, that is an indication that we need to give out more of the Gospel seed.

c. If you lack friends, give more of your friendship away. Proverbs 18:24

In whatever area we give, Jesus has promised that we will receive **more than we give** and **according to how much we give.**

C. **Bountiful sowing leads to bountiful reaping**. 2 Corinthians 9:6

Like the previous laws, this law can be both positive and negative. Bountiful sowing, whether of the spirit or of the flesh, results in bountiful reaping. However, the primary emphasis of this law in Scripture is positive. Whether we are speaking of **material goods**, **spiritual service or personal investments into the lives of others**, the more bountifully we sow, the more abundantly we will receive.

2. The Basis for this Law

A. **God's character**

1. This law is rooted in the fact that it is God's nature to give.

2. The Bible states that we can expect God to be generous with His blessings. Ephesians 3:20 tells us that God is able and desires to do for us:

    a. ALL that we can ask or think.

    b. ABOVE all that we can ask or think.

    c. Exceedingly ABUNDANTLY above all that we can ask or think.

B. **God's plan**

1. Bountiful sowing should always been done according to Biblical principles.

    a. A response of love, not greed. Compare to John 3:16 & 1 John 4:11

    b. Honors God. See Philippians 4:18 *"a sacrifice ... wellpleasing to God."*

    c. Given generously. 2 Corinthians 9:6

God measures what we have sown not by the amount we have given, but by what we have left over. When the widow cast two small coins into the temple treasury while others cast in much, Jesus said, *"This poor widow hath **cast more in**, than all they which have cast into the treasury: for all **they did cast in of their abundance; but she of her want** did cast in all that she had."* Mar 12:43-44

d. Not given as a substitute for giving ourselves.
2 Corinthians 8:5

- Any child will tell you that he would rather have his daddy than a toy.
- It is often easier to give money or things than it is to give our time or service.

2. Though we give knowing that we will receive, that is never our primary motive. We sow to reap to have more to sow, not simply to profit personally.

3. Applying this Law (Ecclesiastes 11:1-6)

You have heard it said that there is a fine line between faith and foolishness. Most of us never have to worry about crossing that line. If anything, we are too cautious when it comes to exercising faith. We don't *"cast our bread upon the waters"* for fear we might go hungry. Not knowing *"what evil shall be upon the earth"* we are more likely to look out for "Number 1" instead giving a portion to seven or eight. The conditions have to be just right before we take what we will call a step of faith.

In this passage, Solomon warns of the danger of being overly cautious, of relying upon perfect circumstances to determine when and how we sow. I find the following truths in this passage.

A. **Life is uncertain but give anyway**.

1. To cast bread upon the waters was one way of describing the shipping industry of that day.
   a. Shipping by sea was a risky business. Boats were fragile, the weather unpredictable. Ships were prone to attack by pirates, to sink in a storm, or otherwise lose their cargo.
   b. Often, it took months for a ship to make the round trip. Once the ship left port, it may not be heard from again until it returned to the dock.
2. Why then would anyone take the risk? Because the profit was greater than the_investment_. a. Often enough, after many days, the ships returned and the shipper's faith was rewarded.
b. Verse 2 could be interpreted, "Send out cargo on seven or eight ships, for you don't know what calamity awaits."
   * The more you send, the more likely it is that some will return.
   * In other words, **the measure of return is determined by the amount put at risk**.

B. **Life is uncertain, but God is always faithful**.

1. Life *is* unpredictable. vs 3-4

a. The clouds may be full of rain, but who can tell where it will fall? Have we not seen Clarksville get an inch of rain when Fort Campbell received none?

b. If the wind blows down a tree, it may fall in any direction – harmlessly onto the street or tragically upon your new car.

c. What Solomon is telling us is that **these circumstances are beyond our control**.

- You waste your time worrying about them.
- You waste your opportunities if you wait for circumstances that are free from risk.

2. We cannot second-guess the ways of God, but we can trust Him to keep his Word and reward our faith. vs 5-6

a. The only way we can come to grips with the uncertainty of life is to sow our seed and trust God with the results – *regardless*.

b. We are to sow morning and evening – at every opportunity – and patiently wait for God to give the harvest.

Don't be stingy with your life. Sow all you can, knowing that you will reap in proportion to the amount sown.

LAW SIX:
WE REAP THE FULL HARVEST OF THE GOOD ONLY IF WE PERSEVERE
Galatians 6:9-10

Verse 9 contains both a **promise** and a **prerequisite**. The promise is, *we shall reap.* The prerequisite is, *if we faint not.* **To receive the full fruit of our labors, we must persevere.** Scripture, life experiences, and nature teach us that we reap the full harvest of the good only through persistent effort. Evil, on the other hand, needs no help to spread and multiply. This is a principle that every farmer understands. A field must be cultivated regularly to provide for conditions that promote healthy growth and fruitful plants. However, weeds will soon overrun what was once a fruitful field if it is left to itself. Complacency or neglect takes its toll on everything. Consider, for example, a new home. It won't stay new looking very long without continual upkeep. In time, the paint will begin to crack and peel. The carpets will get dirty and the linoleum scuffed and scarred. Dandelions and stickers will begin to grow in the yard. Time, use, and the elements will take their toll on your house unless you remain watchful for signs of decay and persistently fight against them.

The same is true in our lives, our homes, and our church because of the many forces that work against the good. Knowing the enemies we face and our own natural tendency to become complacent, Paul commanded us to persevere in well doing until the harvest was reaped.

1. The Certainty of Opposition

A. The Presence of Sin

1. Sin has made our world subject to a principle of decay and death.
> a. Romans 8:20-22 tells us that the world is in a *bondage of corruption* and *the whole of creation groaneth and travaileth in pain together until* this present time.
> b. Hebrews 1:10-12 states that the earth *shall wax old as doth a garment*.
> c. 1 Peter 1:24 declares that *all flesh is as grass, and all the glory of man as the flower of grass. The grass withereth and the flower thereof falleth away.*

2. Because of this principle, we can only reap the harvest of the good through persistent hard work. Genesis 3:17-19
> a. As the ground brings forth thorns and thistles, so life brings forth trials and travail.
> b. Man must labor in the sweat of his brow to "eat bread," and he must do so continually until the

day of his death. So, life only yields the full harvest of the good (whether of things material or spiritual) through persevering labor.

This principle of decay effects every area of our existence. Without persistent hard work, your spiritual life will wither, your family relationships will erode, and the work of Christ will suffer from complacency and neglect.

B. The Person of Satan

In Matthew 13, Satan is presented as opposing the harvest of the good. Through the parable of the sower and the parable of the wheat and tares, we see Satan's methods of opposition.

1. **He works to prevent the good seed from taking root and maturing**. Matthew 13:3-4, 19

   a. In this parable, the seed is the Word of God. The sower is the Lord and, by application, anyone who is involved in spreading the Word of God.

   b. The birds represent the "evil one," Satan and his workers, who snatch away the seed sown in the heart before it can bring forth any fruit.

   - Satan works to keep the lost from believing and obeying the Gospel.
   - He also works to keep Christians from believing and obeying the Word of God.

2. **He sows false seed to grow up alongside the good**. Matthew 13:24-25; 36-39

a. In this parable, we see two sowings:

- That of the man who owns the field, who expects to reap a particular harvest because he has sown "good seed" into his field.
- That of the enemy who sowed seed that would bring no harvest, *only hamper and obstruct the fruitfulness of the good seed.*

b. In the same way, when Satan cannot prevent growth and maturity by snatching the seed away, he works to keep it from reaching its full potential.

- He trespasses into "fields" which should rightfully bring forth a good harvest.
- Out of hatred for God, he sows his seeds of opposition.
- He does it "while men sleep" – when they are not expecting it nor watching for it; by implication, when they are complacent and have let down their guard.

Because of the presence of sin and the person of Satan, with every opportunity to do good (Galatians 6:10), there will be opposition to be faced and overcome.

2. The Command to Persevere – Galatians 6:9-10

A. **The peril of discouragement** *"And let us not be not weary in well doing"*

1. **The word translated weary means "to lose heart," to become discouraged.**
> a. It is human nature to lose the desire to continue because of difficult circumstances or unfulfilled expectations.
> b. This is especially true when results are not immediately apparent; when, in fact, it seems as if our work is unproductive, unappreciated, or unrewarded.

2. **Well-doing – to reap the full harvest of the good – requires continued effort.** Discouragement will cause us to quit before we have reached our goal. Florence Chadwick was the first woman to swim the English Channel in both directions. On July 4, 1951, she attempted to swim from Catalina Island to the California coast. To complicate matters, a dense fog settled over the area that prevented her from seeing more than a few feet ahead. After about 15 hours in the water, and less than a half-mile from her goal, Chadwick gave up. Later she told a reporter, "If I could have seen land, I might have made it."

B. **The prospect of weariness** *"If we faint not"*

1. **The word translated "faint" literally meant to loosen or relax in such a way that a thing became weakened**.

> a. It was used of a bowstring that had lost its tension, thus lessening the efficiency and power of the bow.
>
> b. It was often used of becoming physically weakened through hunger or exhausting labor.

2. **Paul recognized an inescapable truth: well doing often produces emotional and physical exhaustion**. Today, we call it "burn-out."

> a. One reason for this is our good works never seem to have a point of completion.
>
> - Can we ever say that we have finished the work of evangelism?
> - There is no time clock for parents to punch in and punch out; they are on the job 24 hours of the day.
>
> b. Another reason for this is that the good often carries a sense of urgency.
>
> - The word *"opportunity"* in verse ten is the same as the word *"season"* in verse 9. It means **a limited amount of time, a decisive period**.
> - The implication is that we must seize the opportunities given to us to do good because they may not present themselves again.

3. **To avoid fainting, it is vital that we find time for spiritual, physical, and emotional refreshment**.
a. Tired people (emotionally or physically) are less productive, prone to mistakes, and more vulnerable to discouragement and depression.
b. Some have said, "I'd rather burn out than rust out." The problem is, either way you're out.

C. **The promise of the harvest** *"in due season we shall reap"*

1. **"In due season" reminds us that there is a relationship between seedtime and harvest.**
a. We have "opportunities" to do good. When they arrive, it's time to sow.
b. For every opportunity, there is a time appointed for harvest. To miss the former is to lose the latter.

2. **"We shall reap" is God's promise to the faithful and believing.**
a. On this basis, Paul charges us to take the opportunities God gives us. Verse 10
b. Persevering comes from the sure knowledge that God will keep His Word, the time of harvest will arrive, and therefore, our labor is not in vain.

There is a need to persevere in sowing good seed. It is seldom easy, often tiresome, and usually under appreciated. Sometimes, we don't even see the fruit of our labors in this life. We do the sowing, and a future generation reaps. A wonderful illustration of this truth is found in the life of John Wycliffe.

Wycliffe worked hard at giving the world an English translation of the Bible. He wanted a Bible that anyone could read, not just the priests. He was declared an outlaw and a heretic for his efforts. His enemies made no secret of the fact that they sought his life, and Wycliffe had to finish his work while in hiding. When it was finished, there was no printing press, so each copy had to be made by hand. It was a slow and expensive project. Then, less than two years after the first copy was completed, Wycliffe died. Years later, he was so hated by his enemies that they dug up his bones, burned them, and scattered the ashes on the Thames River.

Today, we are the reapers of Wycliffe's harvest. We have the Bible in our hands because he didn't quit in the face of opposition and discouragement. He stayed at the task, which is what we all must do if we expect to reap the full harvest of the good.

www.ingramcontent.com/pod-product-compliance
Lightning Source LLC
Chambersburg PA
CBHW031431250726
48656CB00002B/939